Test Taking Strategies – Proven Methods For Success

Dr. Mitchel Schwindt

C 2014

Singularis Media Group, LLC

Table Of Contents:

Please Take A Moment

Please share a quick review on Amazon after you have had a chance to dive into this book. I have put the best strategies to pen in creating this resource to help motivated students reach new academic heights.

Customer Reviews

★★★★★ (7)
5.0 out of 5 stars

5 star		7
4 star		0
3 star		0
2 star		0
1 star		0

Share your thoughts with other customers

Write a customer review

See all 7 customer reviews

Most Helpful Customer Reviews

2 of 2 people found the following review helpful
★★★★★ **Test Taking Simplified** September 13, 2012
By drbilldean
Format: Kindle Edition | Amazon Verified Purchase

I wish I had this useful book in test taking years It would have cleared the fog that s techniques to help improve performance Dr Bill Dean

Comment | **Was this review helpful to you?** Yes   No

1 of 1 people found the following review helpful
★★★★★ **I wish my students would read this** September 14, 2012
By Daris Howard
Format: Kindle Edition | Amazon Verified Purchase

Though, as a teacher, I wondered if I want my students to read this book, it made m importance of getting rest and proper nutrition before a test. This is especially stron don't remember what they crammed anyway.

Comment | **Was this review helpful to you?** Yes   No

1 of 1 people found the following review helpful
★★★★★ **Great Guide** September 13, 2012

The Reality

If you are reading this, you are someone who is clearly dedicated to improving his or her chance for success.

If you are seeking better grades, acceptance to law or medical school, better decision-making abilities or just want to improve your cognitive skills, please read on.

The fact that you are spending a few moments of your precious time to read this shows that you have the dedication to succeed in the arena where others will consistently fail. You are already miles ahead of the competition.

Introduction

For the last 15 years I have been advising and helping motivated students get results. The academic road is challenging and there are many stumbles along the way.

As a physician, I have endured the arduous journey of rigorous academic study and share with you how to achieve mastery. You will learn to reshape your goals and reach higher in any academic endeavor. It's time to get the grades and exam scores you want and deserve. Don't let the time and effort of studying go to waste due to poor test taking abilities.

The techniques and principles taught are focused for college and university level students, but younger students looking for an early edge in test taking abilities will benefit considerably.

Why You Need To Plow Through This?

Whatever your ultimate destiny, if it is truly worthwhile, will give you substantial challenges to overcome. You will struggle at times, curse/swear, doubt yourself and second-guess yourself at times. But in the end, those of you with true passion and dedication will succeed.

In this book, I share what I have learned over the last 15 years guiding aspiring students to greater heights. I will spare you the tedium of the science and math behind test taking strategies, but instead provide specific techniques, tools and strategies that will increase your exam performance. Erase the dread you may fear when a test is looming large on your academic road.

What You Will Gain

This guide provides specific insight into difficult questions, tools and strategies on how to focus in on the correct answer and how to get into the mind of the examiner. Some students are blessed with the innate ability to zero in on the correct choice, no matter how foreign the subject matter. The rest of us have to rely on cognitive strategies to navigate the forest without getting lost.

This guide will help you do just that, and the end result will be an overall improvement in test scores More simply stated, you will develop the ability to reason through the incorrect choices, score well and stand out from the crowd.

Physiology Matters

This is an overview of some basic concepts in the physiology of testing and studying. Other chapters focus on specifics, such as caffeine; but this chapter provides a general discussion.

The key here is sleep and nutrition. We know that the brain consumes a large amount of glucose, and it gobbles up almost 20 percent of the blood flow the heart pumps out. Think about that: almost 20 percent of all the blood in your body is being used just to fuel your brain to keep it going. Clearly, ignoring the basic physiology of brain function means slighting yourself and losing points on your exam. An athlete needs proper rest, nutrition, and training, and so does your brain.

Try to function when you're hungry, try to study when you're hungry, try to take a test when you feel as if you're starving: not only do you feel poorly, but also your brain probably doesn't have the energy it needs to function optimally and your performance is likely to suffer.

Your brain likes sugar—particularly glucose, which is a simple sugar. But consuming a lot of sugar is not a valid fuelling strategy, because sugars are burned through quickly and cause some physiological spikes. A spike in insulin occurs after sugar intake, and can result in crashing.

A better strategy is to take in whole foods before an exam; consume something that's a good source of carbohydrate and of energy that's going to last through the test. This is especially important when you're taking an important exam that is many hours long, such as a DAT, LSAT, or ACT.

In my opinion, foods that are low on the glycemic index, that are absorbed slowly and stabilize the blood sugar, are a good idea. The mantra I like to use is "Go brown": brown is whole wheat, brown rice, quinoa, things like that. Leave your Mountain

Dew and Diet Coke at home; leave your candy bars in the vending machine. Obviously, if you're crashing and bonking, or just trying to get through an exam, those will give you quick energy; but, as your default strategy, they should be avoided.

Hydration is important. Of course, you don't want to be running to the bathroom every 20 minutes during your exam, but simple dehydration affects physiology immensely. In athletics, just a small amount of dehydration results in a significant decrease in performance. Your brain is basically swimming; it's suspended by cerebrospinal fluid (CSF). The CSF is largely comprised of water and electrolytes. And, like the rest of your body, your brain is sensitive to dehydration. In addition, you tend to feel poorly when you're dehydrated. Most people who are drinking a lot of caffeine and may not be consuming the best diet, such as students, are likely functioning in a chronically dehydrated state with impaired performance.

Sleep is critical. If you're spending every available hour studying before an exam, you're probably depriving yourself of sleep, which will undo at least some, if not all, of the benefit gained from the studying. The lack of adequate sleep interferes with your ability to take tests and perform at a high level.

I know this just from trial and error as an emergency physician. In this field, we're forced to work a lot of shifts and to work nights, and it's well documented that sleep deprivation hurts performance.

Students are often remiss to accept this, but the truth is that cramming and pulling all-nighters does worsen their performance. People who try to pull all-nighters, such as shift workers, particularly emergency doctors, are prone to microsleep: after being up all night, the next day they tend to have periods of microsleep, in which they fall asleep for anywhere from a fraction of a second to thirty seconds, often without even being aware that it has happened. Obviously this is dangerous if you're driving, and it's certainly not helpful if you're trying to get through an exam. Dozing off for five or ten seconds periodically is not what you want to be doing. Rest and keep your mind in sharp condition when it matters the most – exam time.

Getting physically comfortable also is important. Many factors affect your physical comfort during a test, including the type of room, the type of chair, whether the desk is comfortable, whether it's too hot or too cold, the noise level, and so on.

One of the hardest parts about test taking is what I call "the next-door neighbor": you can't predict, and often have no say in, who will be seated next to you. It might be a gum-chewer; a pencil-tapper; a nail-biter; or someone who coughs, has a runny nose, or sighs or groans. Those are all distracting. Learning to take tests in such an environment is one strategy; you could sit in a busy part of your campus, take a practice exam, and see how well it goes. You might be allowed to wear earplugs during your exam. I recommend testing that option in advance; I wouldn't just show up at an exam and try putting in earplugs for the first time: some people are bothered by the sounds and sensations of the earplugs themselves.

Wear comfortable clothes. You don't want to feel tight binding at your waist or hips when you're going to be seated for a long while. If you fidget because you're dressed uncomfortably, you yourself may be that distracting neighbor. Your outfit also should allow you to adjust to changes in temperature, so that you're not too hot or too cold. Be prepared to add or subtract layers to keep comfortable and maintain focus on the exam at hand.

If you have other ideas about what might help you do well on your exam, talk to your instructor ahead of time.

One of my medical school classmates liked to take his exams while lying on the floor. He would find a spot in the corner of the room and lie down to take his test. A little odd, but he consistently ROCKED the exams. His philosophy was that if he could be comfortable and feel like he was not being crowded his thought processes flowed better. I say whatever works. He got the grades he wanted and the competitive residency after med school that other's so badly wanted.

Even if it's a little bit different, you have to do what's right for your body, so talk to your faculty or test proctor. If you're sitting next to a noisy person, or a heater that's turning on and off and distracting you, ask to be moved; there's no harm in asking.

Finally, breathe. When anxious and stressed, many of us often hold our breath or breathe shallowly, which has some negative physiological effects. So take a few periodic deep breaths if you find yourself getting too tense or stressed during exams. Inhale to the count of four, exhale to the count of six, and repeat a few times; often you'll find yourself re-centered, refocused, and ready to get back to the a task at hand, which is successfully completing your exam and getting the grade that you both desire and deserve. This is proven scientifically and the simple act can make all the difference.

Test Taking Anxiety

Let's look at the mental side of test taking and how it applies to studying and to study strategies in general.

Eat, Sleep, and Move: these three concepts are critical not only to academic success, but also to success in life in general.

Proper nutrition and eating are a key element of success that is often overlooked. It can be difficult, especially when you're a student, to go grocery shopping and take the time to make something nutritious. Often, as students, we're eating things that come in wrappers, eating bars, living on the proverbial ramen noodles and diet soda. But we all know that certain foods make us feel a certain way; when you eat a bunch of junk food or fast food, you may not feel as well as when you eat something that was prepared at homc.

Sleep often is overlooked. It comes at a premium: you're busy, you're studying, you're working, you're preparing for exams, you have a social life, and you like to work out or partake of other athletic pursuits. But even just fifteen-minute naps are often enough to rejuvenate and recharge the body, the mind, and the spirit.

Move. It is well documented that sedentary activities are associated with an overall increased risk of death. Many occupations, at least in this country, involve sitting for extended periods. When studying for a degree is your occupation, you're sitting for probably four hours a day in lectures, in addition to the time you spend seated while riding or driving to and from campus, and the many hours you sit while studying. Even those who exercise regularly have an increased risk of early death if they also sit for hours at a time: taking *frequent* breaks to stand up and move—say, every twenty minutes—even if they're brief, is key.

Taking a time-out for a half-hour walk to clear your mind, taking a jog or a run, and participating in an exercise class at the campus recreation center, are all highly valuable—mainly in terms of overall health, but also in terms of the benefits of recharging and restoring your mind so that you can focus again on your academic success. After all, the purpose of your education is to not only to get a degree, but also to develop proficiency for living life.

A close friend of mine in medical school was an avid runner, and spent a lot of time on the treadmill, the stair-climber, or the elliptical machine, going over notes or reading. Getting used to studying while in motion takes a little practice. Another option is an exercise bike; if you like to bike, that's a simple way to get some exercise and take advantage of the chance to study at the same time.

The next topic is a huge one for some students. Don't let test-taking anxiety be a big issue. Let's look at some strategies that I've found helpful with the students I've worked with over the years.

The most basic thing to do is to get help. If you have a test-anxiety problem and you know about it, don't ignore it: get help. There are plenty of resources available on campus—professional resources to help you work through this, tackle it head on, and address it early. Don't just ignore it and hope it goes away, because it never does without proper help, techniques, and strategies to address it. Be proactive as your future depends on it.

Schedule yourself appropriately. Schedule study time, schedule test-preparation time, schedule downtime. Map it all out, so that you're not panicked at the last minute, trying to figure out how to fit it all in.

Visualize success. This is well documented in sports psychology, but also applies to any arena. When you visualize success, no matter the area of your life, the likelihood of your achieving that success is much higher. Picture yourself as having succeeded in preparing for the exam, in taking the exam, in getting a decent score: visualize any of those steps, and especially all of them, and your chances will improve significantly.

I don't want to come across as too otherworldly here; but meditation is a simple strategy that helps, not only with test-taking anxiety but also with anxiety in general. We all operate at a frenetic pace, and it's very difficult to find time to calm down and relax. Take five minutes in the morning, *before* you check your phone or email, to focus and meditate, to take some deep breaths, to appreciate what's around you, to be thankful for what you have—including the chance to pursue higher education, and the fact that you have goals and an inspiring future ahead of you. Bookend that at the end of the day, when the books are put away, the television is off, the computer and phone arc off, by taking a few minutes to breathe and to sit and reflect on what you've accomplished during the day. Reflect on your success and what you're thankful for, and often that will reset your mental clock for tomorrow.

Avoid negativity. We're all prone to negative thoughts. I once read that something like an astounding 40,000 negative thoughts enter a person's mind during a typical day. Try to push those negative thoughts from your mind. When you're studying difficult material, and the thought pops into your head that you're never going to get this, that you're going to perform poorly on the exam, push it out of your mind and focus your attention on the task at hand. Replace the negativity with something better: visualize success. Replace the negative with positive thoughts on how much you have accomplished already. With practice, the positive thoughts will become more the norm.

To an extent, you should also befriend anxiety. Before a musical or athletic performance, or a first date, we're all prone to get butterflies in our stomachs. Just remember that that can be your mind's and your body's way of signaling that you're ready, that you're excited about the task at hand. Understand that some degree of jitteriness is normal. What you're seeking is not the absence of fear, but simply the ability to proceed in spite of the fear.

Don't forget to take a break. This is especially important in certain circumstances. If you're studying, taking practice exams, preparing for a test, and you can't focus and it's just not going well—take a break. You're more likely to achieve your goal after you take a break than you are if you simply muscle your way through. I've seen many students over the years who were tired—perhaps because they were up late the night before, they worked an extra shift to make some extra money, or they stayed out partying too late over the weekend—and trying to force themselves through a three-hour study session, but who in the end really gained very little. Exhaustion saps memory and impairs functioning. Take a break, take a nap, take a walk, and go sit outside, call a friend or call your family. Completely separate yourself from the learning process, at least for fifteen minutes. Often that will be enough to allow you to focus better when you return to your test preparation.

Remember the past. Remember your successes in particular. Many people tend to hang on more to the negative things that happened in their lives, and their failures, than to their successes. Your successes are important to remember and to celebrate. Focusing on your past academic and other success, including exams on which you did well, along with focusing on your innate abilities and skills, is a great way to remember and honor your past. This simple technique allows you to set the expectation in your subconscious mind that you will succeed in the future, on the next test, in the next course and the next semester.

Finally, breathe. I've mentioned this in other chapters, and I'll mention it again here because it's so simple and so important. When we're anxious and tense, we tend to breathe shallowly, and even to hold our breath; this creates a whole host of physiological responses in the body and in the mind. Just taking breaths when you're anxious, stressed, or nervous goes a long way toward releasing the tension, toward dispensing with the pent up anxiety and other emotions. So take a deep breath in and let a deep breath out. You can count. You don't need a mantra; this is not a meditation course: it's just a technique that has proven very successful for many of the students I've worked with over the last several years, and it will help you too.

Test-Taking Myths

In this chapter, we'll examine a dozen test-taking myths that seem to never die.

Myth #1: Smart people are good test-takers. This may be partly true, but tests measure more than innate intelligence. They measure your ability to take tests, your ability to decipher and discern the stem of the question—what the instructor is asking.

There are many unusually smart people who perform poorly on tests. The rest of this chapter is dedicated not only to dispelling the myths, but also to giving you strategies that will help you become a better test-taker.

Myth #2: Tests measure how much you know.

Actually, tests measure how much you can recall, or figure out, at a given point in time; they are not a true measure or reflection of your entire knowledge base or ability to reason.

Many students, discouraged that they've performed poorly on a single test, extrapolate that poor performance into a much larger definition of themselves, such as "I'm just bad at math", I'm not good at chemistry, I don't get this history stuff". Many of the students I work with often need to overcome that mental hurdle. You must understand that sub-par performance isn't necessarily a true measure of what you know or of your ability to succeed as a student. It is a measure at one point in a long line.

Myth #3: Time is key.

The prevalence of this myth is probably the biggest hurdle that gets in the way of good exam performance for the students I've worked with in the last decade. Many of us are laboring under the false belief that brute force is really the only way to prepare successfully for a test or exam. In fact, it's not so much the time you put in, as it is how you allocate that time. Studying efficiently and effectively is different from just studying. We delve deeper into that fact in another chapter; but, here, just know that, in terms of your chance of success, putting in an excessive or inordinate amount of time pales in comparison to study that is efficient and active.

Efficient is getting things done quickly with the least effort. Effective is doing the right things. Know the difference when planning your test preparation strategy.

Myth #4: Cramming is effective.

This one never goes away. I hear it all the time: "I'm going to cram for this test. I'm just going to stay up all night cramming, and then take the test at eight o'clock in the morning and I'm sure I'll do fine." For a *few* people, this *might* work. The probability is that, for you, it won't.

Cramming is sometimes an effective way to store information for a very short period, but it really doesn't lay down any of the neural foundation that constitutes long-term, sustainable memory. There's a chance that this will work for a test on which you're just going to spit out a bunch of data or facts. You will forget much of it by next day and exponentially lose more each passing day.

Most critical coursework builds on itself throughout the semester, throughout the year, and throughout your whole educational career. Cramming, although it may give you superficial success on a particular test, will not have served you well at the end of the semester or at the end of the year, when you find that those long-term memories were never formed. When you go back to review the material, it will be almost as if you're seeing it for the first time. Please, take that to heart. You have lifelong goals; you want a fulfilling career, not just a decent score on a test on a single day in your life. (exceptions: MCAT/LSAT/DAT or similar)

Myth #5: Sleep-studying always works.

We don't hear as much about this as we did in years past, but I still find a few students who believe that this is a reliable way to study.

In sleep-studying, a student records a lecture, and then plays the recording while asleep, in the hope that the material will be absorbed by the subconscious mind and then will be able to be recalled during an exam. Maybe this works for some, but it's a method to be avoided. Listening to a physics lecture while you're trying to sleep is disruptive to your sleep; it interferes with your ability to derive the benefits that restful sleep confers upon your mental functioning when you're awake. In terms of effectiveness, sleep-studying is very low on the technique list of things that actually improve your test performance. It's also cumbersome: who wants to sleep with headphones on? And, if you're just playing it over a speaker, you invite conflict with your roommates.

Myth #6: Studying right before a test is best.

This is related to cramming. Some students wait until the last day or two before a test before they put in the effort to study. Such studying can work to an extent; but, again, it's the repetitious exposure to material over a longer period, and active study methods, that actually lay down long-term neural connections, allowing you to recall the data when you need it.

Myth #7: Pressure works.

This is related to studying right before a test. Some people do study and perform effectively under pressure. Some students wait till the last minute to write a paper and actually do better work then. But, for *most* people, the extra pressure and stress of trying to fit in a study session at the last minute don't work. Instead, this technique causes extra anxiety; it creates a sense of panic; and it changes the physiology in the neural, humoral, and hormonal chemistry in a way that, for most people, reduces their ability to learn effectively. Create a low-pressure environment that fosters an attitude of success.

Myth #8: You should always study in the same place.

Many of us are creatures of habit and like to study in the same place all the time, such as a dorm room, a bedroom, or a specific spot in the library or school. That's O.K. But, in addition to studies showing that this technique doesn't produce better test performance, and indeed can produce worse results than varying your study location.

There is also some pretty interesting evidence showing how the brain processes information and forms memories. A memory is formed not just of a single, specific task, but also from the whole array of sensory inputs that you were experiencing while performing that task. That includes sight, smell, taste, sound, and tactile sensations, along with your sense of what is going on inside your own body, such as hunger, fatigue, and relaxation. Smell may be our strongest trigger both of emotion and of memory; after all, for us and many others species, this sense is a way of gathering information about things in our environment that, though silent, invisible, and too distant to touch, may yet affect our health and safety. You learn more about this concept in the Method of Loci section later.

When you're studying a topic at a specific place in the library, you're building up a neural history in which the information that you're studying is being recorded not in isolation, but in connection with many other sensory inputs from your immediate environment. The smells, the lighting, the mood and atmosphere, and so on are incorporated. All of this information is laid down together, in a neural framework that includes both the topic you're studying and the other sensory inputs.

If, a week later, you review the same material, but in your favorite coffee house instead of the library, you lay down a separate neural framework. It contains the same basic information that you're studying, but in combination with a different set of environmental stimuli—different smells, different lighting, a different mood and atmosphere, even different tastes (if you're eating). The material that you're learning is the same, but your brain will form a separate memory, in a different location, based on the inputs around that information. The common feature of the two memories is the information that you were intentionally studying, which now is recorded in two places, not just one. Essentially, you have a redundant backup system, which improves both your ability to retain the information in your long-term memory and your ability to recall the information when you want it.

It's quite an effective technique. I've used it myself for last thirty years, and I think it's one of the keys to success.

Studying in the same location day in and day out also gets boring. You're stuck in the same spot, and every day seems the same. We know, from a scientific and medical perspective, that the reason why *time*, as you get older, seems to slow down and drag on is that more and more of the situations in which you find yourself are *not new*.

Only *once* can you can ride a bike for the *first* time; no matter how many more times you ride a bike, none of those will ever be another first time. When you're a child, so much of what you do and are exposed to is new: new sights, new smells, new trips, new foods, new friends, new houses, new schools—everything is different. Everything changes rapidly, and that lays down a lot of memories.

Think back to childhood and, I'm sure, you can pull out many vivid, intense memories. If you look back on your memories from within the last year, there probably are many days that just blur together. That's because the situation and environment changed very little; you were in the same classroom, or the same spot in the library studying, and so the formation of those memories is much different and can be much less easy to recall.

Myth #9. You should change your answers.
The old idea here was that, if you're unsure of an answer, you should just take your first guess, stick with it, leave it alone, and not change it. But we now know, from several large studies, that there is some benefit to changing your answers. Students can go back and rethink, and often they end up changing an incorrect answer to a correct answer.

I think that's a pretty interesting finding, but that it must be interpreted with a word of caution. Many of the students I work with sometimes panic. They're trying to get into a program that requires impeccable grades, and they're sort of freaked out about getting a B or a C on an exam. And so they go back and rethink—and over-think—questions; and, often in a moment of panic, they let that emotion cloud their judgment, and they end up changing correct answers. Unless you have a clear idea about why your first answer is wrong, you should leave it alone.

Myth #10: Anxiety comes from lack of preparation, and it predicts failure.

While it's true that those who are woefully unprepared, and who definitely will fail, may well feel anxious before and during an exam. The fact is that many students who are well prepared and who score well are also anxious at test time.

Anxiety does not necessarily say anything about your level of preparation or your chance of success. It's the same as in athletics. Before an event, a little anxiety is good. It means that you're excited, that you're prepared. Sometimes it means you're just fearful of poor performance. Don't let the mere *fear* of failure become a *guarantee* of failure; it almost never is. Instead, take a deep breath; breathe in for a count of four, and exhale for a count of six. Do that a few times, and get yourself focused. It only takes 1-2 minutes. If you need to, get up, walk around, and get a drink.

Create a pre-test ritual as a way to deal with the anxiety of test taking. If it's really a big problem for you, and you tend to panic or freeze or perform poorly despite a very solid knowledge base, then it's time to stop in at your school's career-services office or counselor's office for help. You can find specific techniques to deal effectively with test anxiety.

Myth #11: IQ is predictive.

This is my absolute favorite.

A high score on an intelligence test is no guarantee that you will do well on any other test. Besides the requisite knowledge, it really comes down to will power. The desire and drive to succeed are **twice** as predictive of academic success as IQ alone is. This has been proven scientifically!

Take that to heart: you don't have to be the brightest star to perform exceptionally well. It just comes down to willpower, desire, and drive.

Myth #12: Stimulation is the answer.

Actually, too much chemical and environmental stimulation can hurt your performance.

There is evidence that caffeine can boost learning, but that's only to a point. I think the current trend, especially in Western society, is toward an overreliance on these types of stimulation. Many of us are stimulated almost 24 hours a day: we're drinking coffee in the morning, guzzling energy drinks throughout the day, sipping a Diet Coke while we study; our phones are buzzing, and there's a lot of noise. Stimulation up to a point is beneficial, but beyond that it's detrimental.

Do you have headaches or palpitations, or feel jittery or anxious all the time? Take a closer look at how much caffeine and other excessive stimulation you are exposed to.

Conclusion.

Don't get swept up in the myths and hyperbole. Everyone has his or her own methods of taking tests and of preparing for them. Some of these methods, no matter how prevalent in the popular consciousness, are unlikely to work. Other methods, even though they're not sexy, really improve your chance of success.

Learn about yourself; learn your physiology. Learn what works for you, and stick with it. Don't try to adapt your study habits or test-taking methods to whatever just happens to work for a friend who maybe has scored better than you in the past. Everything is individual. Square pegs still don't fit it into round holes.

Brute force is not going to work for most people. Students are busier than ever and often don't have a lot of time. You may have a job, you want a life and you have friends. Don't rely on using all your time just to study. You're only human. You're going to make mistakes. You may perform poorly from time to time, and that's fine. Just learn from the poor performances and move on. Don't immediately sweep aside the bad experience, but first remember that there are many aspects of a poor performance that are worth examining.

Was it due to?
- Poor preparation
- Poor sleep
- Anxiety
- Some other factor
- Social stress, a breakup with a significant
- Job stress

Learn from it, and then move on to your next shot at success.

Test Taking Tips: The Ground Floor

Key Elements

You need to pay close attention to key words.

These words must call you to attention. Examples are as follows: but, except, most likely. If you are a speed-reader and skim over these qualifiers you will get the question WRONG.

Note any RED FLAGS! If something sounds impossible, it most likely is the wrong choice. Apply some common sense when narrowing down answers and your score will jump up with that simple consistent plan alone.

Eliminate all wrong answers right away. Cross them out, mark them off, whatever you need to do so that the elements in that choice don't climb back into your consciousness as you ponder the correct answer.

If ANY part of an answer is WRONG---

--- the whole answer is WRONG.

I have often noticed that highly intelligent students fail when they second guess themselves or spend too much time trying to justify why an answer choice containing some true fact could be the correct choice. If any part is wrong the ENTIRE answer choice is incorrect. Don't let yourself be misled by temptation. Stop the internal debate. Don't try and guess or second-guess that a partially correct answer is the right option. How many questions start with: "Pick the answer that seems mostly correct"? Exactly none...unless the exam writer suffered a mild head injury while preparing the exam questions.

Guessing is OK!

Don't fail to try. There is no penalty for guessing. If you are a slow methodical test taker, mark down an answer BEFORE moving on to the next question. Don't be caught at the end, running out of time only to find yourself marking "C" for all those questions you didn't answer the first time around. There is no penalty for guessing wrong. Not even hazarding a guess is a sure strategy to perform poorly. I'll talk more about random guessing later and why "C" is not a wise choice.

Beware of the Wordy or Unfamiliar

If an answer choice is excessively word dense or seems unfamiliar, it most likely is WRONG. Instructors often try to draw you in by impressive sounding phrases that contain some elements you are familiar with and sprinkle in portions that you know very little about. Look for the choice that contains facts you are familiar with and know are factual and correct.

All, None & Never

The reality is that unless you are dealing with hard science or math, the above qualifiers should disqualify the majority of answers. Beyond the laws of the universe, very few things follow the dictums – Always, None & Never.

Go For The Gold

Always chose the Gold Standard answer. If the particular topic has an industry standard, rote fact/formula or similarly undisputable fact, always select that answer. Let's face it: the Law's of Physics and its unique formulas will guide you to the "Golden" answer.

More on Common Sense

Statements that seem outdated, dangerous, harmful or just plain stupid are just that. The reality is that after years of writing questions, it becomes harder and harder to develop incorrect choices. If it is plainly ignorant, politically or morally unsettling it is wrong. Give yourself the credit you deserve and rely on common sense judgment as part of the decision making process.

The Most Common Simple Mistakes

Highly Intelligent Students Make

Not reading the question carefully

This is so simple, but it goes without fail that many test takers misread or stop reading the actual question prematurely.

Miss a simple qualifier such as: not, all, except, all of the following EXCEPT, none of the following except.....You get the point! Miss one simple qualifying word and you will get the question wrong. Take the extra second or two and read the entire question.

Second guessing yourself

Instincts are there for a reason. Often the "gut" is correct. If you have no clue to the answer, go with your gut instinct. More often than not you'll pick the correct answer. If cross off those answers that you know are partially incorrect and still have no clue let your GUT help guide you.

Not answering the question asked

Asked and answered. That is what you will hear in legal circles. Pay close attention to what the question is ASKING. You may know a few details about the various choices, but focus on what the question is asking / wanting / guiding you towards.

Often challenging material is loaded with terms, definitions and other confusing statements. Most of this is designed to throw you off the track. If you focus on the specific question at hand, you can often eliminate several of the choices right off the bat.

Read into the questions you have no CLUE about and see what they are asking for and you most likely can make an excellent educated guess. Eliminating 2 of 4 choices just significantly improved the odds of getting the question right. Every point counts in the end no matter how or why you chose the correct answer.

Not pacing yourself

Some examiners start of with crazy ridiculously hard questions to throw you off the track. Don't let this fluster you. Not everyone or every test writer plays fair.

Don't dwell on questions you have ZERO clue about.

Maybe you didn't read that chapter, study that topic or even bother to crack your book. Don't sweat it. Examiners develop questions and portions of a particular exam with that strategy in mind. Push on and FINISH the exam. There are no penalties for guessing. An incorrect answer scores the same as NO Answer. Not hazarding a guess if foolish.

If a particular professor always starts off an exam with ridiculously hard questions, skip to the middle or end of an exam and work backwards. There is no

RULE that states start with #1 and the go on. That is how we all first learned to take exams way back in grade school, but feel free to improvise when necessary.

No matter where you start, just please remember to answer each question. Even if you reserve the last 5 minutes of an exam period to go back and fill in all the little bubbles you left blank, you will be better off that those who became flustered and lost concentration. Remember that the first horribly written questions are at times placed just to test your abilities and skill as a test taker.

Picture Questions

Certain topics or questions cannot be answered without specific knowledge of a picture, slide, photo or whatever media the examiner chooses. Realize that often the question can be answered WITHOUT even looking at the picture. Try and decide on the most likely answer based on the stem of the question. At times the photos or images reproduced in exams are subpar and would be difficult to interpret even with the help of an expert. Don't fixate on trying to decipher blurry or poorly reproduced images. Rely on the wording of the question and make an educated choice.

Calculations

OK. You are on your own here! Sorry! You will have to get a feel for what a particular instructor feels is important.

The best strategy is to flat out ASK!

Excuse me Mr. Professor smart person, "Would you like us to know all the formulas you presented over the last semester or how do you suggest one best prepare for the FINAL exam?"

You will be amazed at how often they just TELL you the best-kept SECRET of any exam. It is often there for the asking.

If you meet a stonewall, just say thank you and

move on. Rush home and jump on Facebook or whatever social media you use and ask what previous students have to offer. Ask around in the class, someone likely has a handle on what types of formulas or calculations are generally needed. You may even come up with some old exams to study and you will have the front row seat to how a particular instructor develops their test questions.

Guessing

You just read the KEY.

GUESS.

If you have no clue, if not even a cursory neuron fires when you read a question, done flagellate over the answer options. GUESS and MOVE ON. Save your time and energy; spend it on questions you can actually decipher.

As an advisor and faculty member, I am shocked at the number of students who perform POORLY because they don't even bother to hazard to a guess. Don't fall into this trap. Mark an answer for EVERY question even if you have not a single clue to the answer. Leave nothing blank. Some instructors reward creativity and occasionally humor. If time permits, you can return to these questions and utilize some of the other techniques shared in this book.

General Test Taking Advice

Pick the midranges.

For example: 20%, 50% and 80% are your friends.

Guessing is not penalized.

Don't waste time; take your best guess and move on.

B & D are the best options if you have no clue.

This is proven mathematically. I won't go into the boring details, but it is your best option.

How foolish does "C" seem as a choice?

Well, if you skip over 10 True/False questions where A/B are the only logical choices, "C" makes you not only look like an idiot, but also KILLS your score.

Your first guess is usually right

There is a reason mother nature, God or whatever you believe in gave you INSTINCT. Ignore it at your peril.

Math/Calculations

The majority of placement exams have some questions dealing with problem solving that incorporates an equation or two. These invariably involve simple math and round numbers. You will likely not have a calculator present, hence the simplicity.

Don't second guess yourself and try to come up with a crazy complex math solution to a simple problem.

Check your units carefully. Don't waste a lot of time on these questions. If you cannot recall the relevant formula, then make your best educated guess and move on.

Introduction to Question Development

Every question contains a stem (the question asked) and several incorrect answer choices (foils). Most examinees tend to focus on the stem, but the exam writers will tell you that the foils MAKE the exam.

Creating believable foils is a more difficult proposition than writing the actual question.

"C" is most often the wrong GUESS. I want to reiterate this point from the last section.

If you can't narrow down any choices, guess B or D as a better guess. This is unless you are certain either of those is incorrect.

Facts

Facts and factoid questions directly sample your knowledge. Some of these types of questions will be very good, precise and focus on what you should know with solid confidence. Others are trivial. Don't spend a lot of time of these trivial questions because most often thought rarely helps. Take your best guess and move along to the next question.

In Parts

One Parters

These types of questions generally provide a scenario in which you must decide what the examiner is after and then choose from similar entities. It is imperative that you read the stem carefully. Remember to apply all the above rules. For example, if part of an answer is wrong, all of it is wrong. Don't talk yourself into selecting a partially correct answer. There will always be the Red Herring choice.

These little foils have relevance to the topic at hand, but are often slightly obscure. You will often know the name but little else about the particular foil. Most often these are the incorrect choice. Test writers place them knowing that a fair number of you will choose this answer for a variety of reasons. I should have studied X, I skipped that day, it must have been covered in the lecture that I missed; therefore, it must be the correct answer. You feel all happy inside but the reality is a master question writer fooled you.

Two Parters

This type of questions requires you to draw a conclusion first. Based on that conclusion, you will be presented with a variety of choices. These are often called second order questions or secondary questioning.

Take this one step further and you have a 3-part question. These show up with frequency depending on the level of course you are involved. These higher level questions take a bit more time to answer, but if you apply the above strategies you can be successful. Even narrowing the choices down by 1 or 2 greatly improves your odds beyond chance alone.

Don't let yourself get frustrated or angry that some professor has developed what seems to be unfair or provides an undue challenge. This is where the

GOLD lies. Take a moment to really put forth an educated and calculated guess. Get even a few of these right and your exam scores will consistently improve.

Faculty note that students consistently perform less well on these types of questions for a variety of reasons. Don't let haste, frustration or insecurity and lack of attention to details be your downfall. You can guess intelligently on these types of questions and push up your test results. Make consistent effort from first to the very absolute last question.

Information vs. Data Concepts

The stem of this question type contains a tremendous amount of data and information to sift through. Much of it is irrelevant, and within the stem are the camouflaged critical pieces of data that will suggest the obvious correct answer.

These questions frustrate even the most skilled test

taker due to the length of time it takes to sort through the stem of the questions. It may help to read all of the answer choices first before reading the stem. This will provide you with the framework of what the examiner is seeking for an answer. Focus, push through the static and find the real data that is important to solve the question.

You can cross out irrelevant and distracting parts of the stem to better grasp how the information presented relates the answer choices.

Get Inside The Mind Of Your Prof!

After a semester of listening to a professor or instructor lecture and during any 1:1 meetings, you should have a pretty good understanding of their communication style. Do they joke? Use sarcasm? What types of questions do they ask during lectures or lab sessions?

Some professors lead you right up to the answer, while others create a cryptic maze of unimportant detracting facts. It's your job from day ONE to begin to assess what type of communication style your teacher or professor possesses.

Another valuable resource is all those that have gone before you. Instructors will develop a reputation for being a certain type of exam writer. Some classes are by default notoriously difficult – Organic Chemistry, Calculus, etc. Others are more straightforward and involve mostly memorization of facts. Hunting down some old exams will provide a valuable clue on what type of tests a particular instructor likes to create.

Foils

These will get you; they get everyone from time to time. A strategy that will greatly improve your exam success is the following:

As you go through a particular section of coursework or studying your notes in preparation for an exam, make a running list of facts or terms that you are struggling with, don't understand or simple cannot grasp. Solve these foils and put the issue to rest.

By developing the FOILS list, you will have a simple **last minute** study guide that will allow you to make correct choices, avoid being drawn it to the foil and elevate your exam scores consistently.

Research/Test Questions

At times examiners slip in these types of questions. After all, they are the ones developing a huge pool of questions for exams to come in the future. I'm not saying faculty are lazy, but we all know that tests and questions are recycled.

Examiners slip in research or test questions to assess concordance, test foils and the perfect exact wording of questions. These questions provide a buffer between the examinee and the new test questions. Questions that seem impossible despite your firm grasp on a topic may fall into this category. Don't sweat them. Do you best and continue. These questions are designed to introduce new concepts, new research and new concepts.

Foils - Killer Foils - Feel The Pain!

No quality exam can be complete without quality foils. Many foils are beyond challenging because you may not remember anything about the foil. The foils may or may not be the right choice, but the reality is that this type of foil destabilizes your decision making process. These are the KILLER FOILS.

Depending on the subject matter, KILLER FOILS are too good to pass up for test writers. There are a limited number of foils for any given subject. Some basic knowledge of these entities goes a long way towards your success.

You need to learn some basic facts about these killer foils so that you can resist the temptation to select these deceptive answers when they are wrong and pick them when they are correct.

I know this is painful, but face reality. You are striving for something that the majority of your friends and acquaintances will never accomplish.

Memory Palace / Method of Loci

Loci Memorization

The Loci method of test preparation dates back to Ancient Greece. It is said that, while Scopas was hosting a party, the palace collapsed, crushing many of his guests beyond recognition. Shortly before the collapse, Simonides of Ceos, a poet at the party, had just left the building. By using this memory technique, he was able to identify the dead on the basis of their locations at the banquet table. The Latin for *locations* is *loci*, hence the name of the method, which is also called the *Memory Palace*.

To use this technique, begin by thinking of a place that you know very well. It might be your childhood home, your dorm, or your apartment. It must be a place whose parts you know in detail. Think of the parts of this location in a specific, logical sequence.

For example, you might begin by envisioning how you would drive up to the house, and then where you would park. As you approach the door, what does it look like? Where is the doorbell or the lock or the light? Think of the sequence of steps you would use to get inside. Then, what do you see when you first get in the door? Where do you hang your coat? Continue moving in a logical, easily memorable sequence as you head farther inside. The most easily memorable path is probably the one you naturally follow every day.

The next step is to picture the items you're trying to memorize, in their proper order, in the various parts of the location that you've been thinking of. For example, if the first place you have in mind is the specific spot where you always park your car in the driveway, assign the first item to be memorized to that location. Assign the next item to one of the locations that you would pass as you moved toward the front door. Continue this process, matching each item to be memorized, in sequence, to the elements of the familiar place. The idea is that you visually link the unfamiliar objects to a common-sense sequence of objects with which you're already familiar. Each area in the location that you have in mind should contain just one or two of the items that you need to memorize.

Of course, if you're memorizing biology, facts, or historical dates, it is a little more challenging to make the links between the data and the physical environment. You need to be creative in assigning facts: perhaps an important biological process, or historical event, takes place on the front step, while another occurs in the coat closet. The process is easier if you establish a deeper, more vivid link between the data you have to memorize and the locations you're picturing.

Let's say that you must memorize this sequence: keys, apple, shoes, wallet, and book. You pull in to the driveway and take the *keys* from the car; that's an easy association. Next, you approach the door, which is red; if you give the *apple* an additional trait, the color red, you can more easily tie it mentally to the door. Once inside, you remove your *shoes*. After that, you go to the kitchen, where you set your *wallet* beside the phone. Phonebooks are often kept near telephones, so you can tie the phone not only to *wallet* but also to *book*.

You may find it worthwhile to consult some of the many resources that offer more-detailed examples of how to use this very powerful system. Countless people have used it for thousands of years. I've used it for decades, because I find it a great way to memorize a lot of data. Rote memorization with this technique is much easier than with brute force.

How to Use Practice Questions

There are several schools of thought about practice questions, and I want to share my take on why they're important and what you can gain from using them.

Of paramount importance is the fact that practice questions allow you to gauge your level of learning, your degree of understanding. You can use them to assess your mastery of the material. Going along with this is the fact that they also can boost your self-confidence—or crush it.

Generally, I believe practice questions should be done only after you believe you have studied the material enough to have mastered it. Then the practice questions can help you gauge whether that perception is correct.

If it quickly becomes apparent, from doing the practice questions, that you have not mastered the material, go back and study more before you return to the questions.

Using practice questions before you have mastered the material can give you a very negative image not just of your progress, but also of your whole being, which can crush your self-confidence and have far-reaching, long-lasting effects. That is one reason why you shouldn't use practice questions until you believe you are likely to do well on them.

Another reason is that, when you use the questions prematurely, they fail to establish the links in the material. When you learn a topic *first* by other means, it creates certain connections in your thought process, neural connections in the brain and mind and memory. When the practice questions come *after* that initial learning, using the questions can help strengthen those links, solidifying the learning and allowing more connections to be made.

Practice questions also are useful as a preview of the style of exam you will take, especially if the practice questions or old tests come from the same instructor whose class you're taking. In this case, you can see how the instructor writes, how the questions are constructed, how answers are phrased.

In the case of multiple-choice questions, you can look at the incorrect answer options and see what distinguishes them from the correct answers. Here, I mean not just the fact that one answer is correct while the others are incorrect, but also the distinguishing traits in the word choice, the semantics, and so on. You'll find clues about the style of incorrect answer options that the instructor offers. While eliminating wrong answers according to these criteria, rather than according to their factual incorrectness, doesn't show that you've mastered the material, it can help you score better on the exam.

Familiarizing yourself with these points of instructor style can also keep you from being thrown off by distractions that might make you choose an incorrect answer even when you know the material. It's important to examine not just *whether* you answered a question right or wrong, but also *why*. Was it a matter of misreading the question? Not answering the question asked? Misinterpreting some data in the stem of a multiple-choice question? Both when you answer correctly and when you answer incorrectly, there's a variety of clues that you can gain about the style of exam, and about how you take it. Knowing where you commonly fall short can help you correct yourself more systematically.

Practice questions also can help with pacing. For that purpose, I recommend doing larger blocks of questions, as opposed to answering just one or two and then taking a break or moving on to something else. By learning to get into a rhythm and establish a flow for a particular type of question and type of material, you'll go a long way in terms of preparing for the actual exam.

You can use practice questions to develop positive, constructive habits. This is helpful especially for students who struggle with timing, pacing, being able to finish the exam in the allotted time. Sit down with a block of, say, 25 or 50 practice questions, and then set a timer and just work toward your goal. Learn how to move on when a question poses too much of a challenge; this means both (1) learning to identify such questions and (2) learning how to let go emotionally, how to acknowledge defeat, so that you can move on and have plenty of time for the questions that you *can* correctly answer. During these practice sessions, develop a technique of marking questions for later review, so that you can come back to the more challenging ones if you have time after finishing the easier parts of the exam; knowing that you can come back to them later should make it easier for you to let troublesome questions go for the moment.

Practice questions can help you develop your skill in *reading* questions. The stem is the critical part of all questions. Successful students spend about 75 percent of their time reading and analyzing the stem, and then the other 25 percent in deciding among the answer options. When you read the stem, separate the important from the distracting; the stem itself can contain facts that are there merely as a foil, to trip you up. Only after you've read the stem and have come up with a plausible answer should you begin reading the answer options. If none of the options matches your initial answer and you can't quickly identify and resolve the discrepancy, mark the question for later review and move on to the next one.

Finally, you may find that the practice questions give you additional material to learn—material that was not presented elsewhere or that you didn't read or study, but which is evident in the questions themsclvcs.

My opinion, based on many years' experience, is that using practice questions is an essential element of test preparation. The students I've worked with tend to devote a significant amount of time to practice questions, particularly when they've finished studying and they believe they've mastered their notes or lecture materials. So go ahead and avail yourself of the extremely valuable benefits of working with practice questions.

Pegs, Chunks, and Acrostics: Other Memorization Techniques

This chapter covers three more memorization techniques. Some students swear by them, while others who have tried them just hate them. You'll have to experiment to see whether they work for you.

The first is the **peg** system, is said to have been devised around 1879 in England. It's good for memorizing a list that must be kept in sequence, and can be used for other lists as well. Each "peg" in the system is one of the whole numbers, which you follow in numerical order: one, two, three, four, etc.

The first step is to assign a *peg word* to each peg. Any word will do, but it's better if the word describes something that you can easily visualize and if the word rhymes with the number. For example, "gum" almost rhymes with "one" (you could also use "gun"), "shoe" rhymes with "two", "tree" rhymes with "three", and "door" rhymes with "four". It's easy to picture gum, a shoe, a tree, and a door; and the rhyme strengthens the association between the particular peg word and its number.

Whatever you visualize, get a clear picture of it in your head. If you rhyme "gum" with "one", be clear about the image of the gum. Is it pink? Is it a long stick of gum, a chunk, or a chewed wad? If you rhyme "shoe" with "two", is it a running shoe or a dress shoe?

You can strengthen the association by doing a quick drawing of each of the peg words in association with its number. Draw the gum, then the shoe, the tree, the door, and so on.

To use the technique to memorize your list, you vividly picture an association between the peg word and the item that must be memorized. Let's say you must memorize this sequence: milk, bread, eggs, and cheese. You might imagine a piece of gum stuck to a milk carton; you could picture a shoe crushing a loaf of bread, or the bread tucked inside the shoe; and you might envision a tree full of eggs and a door made of cheese.

You may find it easier to commit these images to memory if you develop the sequence into a story or scene. For example, instead of just a door made of cheese, perhaps you have a friend who is a Green

Bay Packers fan, and maybe this friend is knocking at your door while wearing a cheese hat.

There are several variations on the system, which are easy to find if you look up "peg system". Some of them make the technique useful for very large sequences, such as a hundred items and even a thousand. Give them each a try and see which ones work for you.

The next technique is **chunking**, often used with numerical data. It doesn't take much to describe this system: a long list of individual items to be memorized is simply grouped into a shorter list of "chunks" of data.

For example, if I slowly say to you ten individual numbers and then ask you to repeat the whole list, you may have trouble: 1—0—9—7—2—3—8—5—4—6. Ten individual pieces of information are a lot to handle. But what happens if I give you just three chunks? The same ten digits could be 109, 723, 8546, with the individual components of each chunk being uttered in quick succession: "one-o-nine", "seven-two-three", "eight-five-four-six". It's much easier to recall and repeat, isn't it? We used to do this all the time with phone numbers, before speed dial. You could also phrase the numbers as "one-o-nine", "seven twenty-three", and "eighty-five forty-six".

Either way, these short sequences of chunks are much easier not only to recall in short-term memory but also to commit to your long-term memory.

Finally, there's the *acrostic* technique, commonly used by medical students. A simple example of this comes from music, where the notes for the lines of the treble clef are, from bottom to top, E, G, B, D, and F. Music students use these single letters as the initials for the five words of a short sentence, such as "Every Good Boy Does Fine".

Of course, we're usually trying to remember more than a sequence of letters. In those cases, you can take a sequence of words that are not particularly memorable on their own, condense them to just their initials, and then use those initials to begin the words of a more memorable sentence.

For example, five of the cranial nerves are olfactory, optic, oculomotor, trochlear, and trigeminal. The initials of these, in order, are O, O, O, T, and T. You might turn that into something like "Oh, oh, oh, to touch!" A little silly, a little risqué, but it's easy to picture, and easy to remember.

There you have three more techniques. Much learning involves rote memorization; these techniques can make the process faster and easier, and the results longer lasting.

Parting Words

Unfamiliar or wordy information is usually wrong.

Be careful with the following: All, Never, None, Always. Unless you are dealing with Hard Science these answers are often wrong.

Read every question carefully

Don't second-guess yourself.

Answer the question asked. Pay attention to what is being asked.

Pace yourself.

Always choose an answer for every question.

Best of LUCK! You have made it this far and it is clear that you have a burning desire to be successful. This is the 4th edition of this book and I know you will put these tools to use in mastering your personal exam strategy and achieve amazing results.

Project You

We all have parts of our lives that we wish were better. Finding the time and techniques to improve is challenging as we strive for self actualization.

I've partnered with experts from all realms of life to help you optimize your health, performance and longevity. This project dives into complex issues such as financial freedom, productivity, functional medicine and bio-hacking, and much more.

Head over to the blog to find out more:

http://MitchelMD.com

Project You

Integrating Change

Mitchel M.D.

Mitchel Schwindt, M.D.

Other Excellent Resources:

Test Taking Strategies: Tips From A World Class Tutor

Test Taking Success For All Students – Even Those With ADD

What Smart Students Know

www.ingramcontent.com/pod-product-compliance
Lightning Source LLC
Chambersburg PA
CBHW051234090426
42740CB00001B/23